PINE TO SOUND

PINE TO SOUND

NANCY KUHL

Published in the United Kingdom in 2015 by Shearsman Books Ltd
50 Westons Hill Drive
BRISTOL BS16 7DF
www.shearsman.com

Shearsman Books Ltd Registered Office
30-31 St. James Place, Mangotsfield, Bristol BS16 9JB
(this address is not for correspondence)

ISBN 978-1-84861-412-3

DESIGN Megan Mangum, Words That Work
AUTHOR PHOTO Michael Marsland
COVER Auguste Rodin, *Cambodian Dancer*, 1906

ACKNOWLEDGEMENTS

Grateful acknowledgment is made to the editors of the following magazines in which some of these poems have appeared or are forthcoming: *A Public Space, Colorado Review, Denver Quarterly, Dream the End* (with thanks to Dan Beachy-Quick), *Drunken Boat, FreeVerse, Gathering the Tribes, Jerry, Kiosk, Pleiades Review, Sentence, TAB: The Journal of Poetry and Poetics, Web Conjunctions,* and *Windsor Review.* Some poems herein appear in *The Nocturnal Factory* or *Little Winter Theater,* published by Ugly Duckling Presse (special thanks to Garth Graeper). I am grateful to the MacDowell Colony for a residency during which some of these poems were written and to the Boomerang Fund for Artists for a grant that supported the completion of *Pine to Sound.* For their care and attention to this work, their friendship and humor, thanks also to Cathy Eisenhower, Anna Leahy, Megan Mangum, Caitlin Mitchell, and Elizabeth Willis. My deepest gratitude and love as ever to Richard Deming.

.

TABLE OF CONTENTS

Echo's Voice

barefoot and stricken and stumbling
I stutter when you ask at your very
command all the same I let ferocity
creep in at the edges I bark and bawl
until I'm hoarse and irrelevant ready
to slip back into the dark hollow
my throat this is waiting and
won't you just say it this is muddled
desire repeating itself turning bone
to stone to air to silence spine and
hip my square collarbone when
did we become only sharp and
shattered utterance fierce signals
in the shifting center wings waves pages
perhaps it would be better to stop
here to quit before nothing is left but
soaring cruel and compelling *come in*
we continue we splinter we slide
in treacherous sequence echo speaks
first return returning refrain resounding
voice voice voice and oh how I listen

I

Morning Provisional

It might collapse at any moment, the room;
might come apart at the seams. Drifts in mist

in rain; wind shook everything, almost shook
everything loose. A man on the radio says

vulnerability assessment says *gap analysis.*
Or he calls: years-away voice. Tilting

precarious above the street. Carry on
at late morning coffee, hover over the paper,

tabled. Already it's clear how each story
ends. Trees knock branches to glass; wasps

let themselves in without asking. And letters
pile by the door in luminous envelopes.

There is fracture and there is repair. Call or
letter; riddle or time machine. Weeks of storm

and uncertainty and now splintering sun
delivered through clouds. A bell, a cue,

the hinge in the narrative. Where pieces
came together. The phone might be

an instrument of desire or a means of
containment; a letter might be a compass.

When it turns back on itself like this, the sky
says *look away; pretend the end is not upon you.*

Talking Points

Wasps through the crumbling casement, droning
and sudden, like riddles spilling from gaps
  between ribs;

well-dressed walls mimic they camouflage they
telescope: plaster split open where the nails went in;

and again and always you plot by suggestion you
  parallel you
shimmer bright you eventually you finally give way;

photograph of a trim and toothless jungle,
  unkept promise
of a wild atmosphere—how it cuts me decisively loose;

nevertheless you continue, you calculate axis
  and distance
and revolution in minutes in hours (there is no
  other way);

then evening finds us (oxygen blooming storm
  black and
heaving threat); it owns what we said to the last
  sentence:

in this room and certain others fists of lightning break
  open and
rain falls in fervent curtains when I close the door
  behind me.

Conflagration

All at once. What do they say? One fell swoop. *All my pretty ones.* You take it in. I remember the conflagration and your causal interest in the ashes. Hush before the blaze; crisp instant demanding heat. Then I recognized your ambition. Trap carefully laid; so far and wide the days that devised it. In this moment, in our private nostalgia for Tuesday, we weary, we reach, we want with might to shatter. Flames confirm our sense that something was about to happen. Is about to happen. More. Daily anticipation. All the same that iridescent, that instantaneous. And more. Embers smolder and smoke, ignite. And still here we are both breathing. Even wrecked, the boundaries mark something. I haven't forgotten what your eye can do.

On Hearing Voices

The hand and what we catch hold of. Point
always to the far edge. And the story
of bones perfectly and cleanly

broken. Now the clear blue context
rushes, slips through, spilling
away in streams in swift rivulets.

— —

Once-familiar sound, distinct
and distant as bells at the hour.

This recognition, this broken-
lung return finds every patience
in the living body. Fills even
the otherwise agreeable mouth.

— —

The dead keep talking, each syllable
churns and grinds, persuasive as axel
and singing gears, steady as a machine.

— —

Empty apartment where moss
and mushrooms grow greenblack and
brown in the decay of the refrigerator.

Tree limbs break in, reaching.
                    The final crumbling
is hastened by even the smallest noises
setting down their unbearable weight.

— —

Time has fingers
like knives. Talking
and not harmless;
the ghost at the edge
of everything.

And the nervous system crackling.

Fray

my suspended second story

tilts keen and madly swaying

wild a ship's transom untethered

this is winter so like a tear

a worn patch in the fabric

skin showing through

the day endures tangle

bears consequence and the room

the lopsided room ready

to crack open wide this is

winter unraveling and if I am

almost pinned by skeletal light

by cross-pane shadows the hour

at least is set steady stretched

tight and unyielding by sure strokes

cast slender those dark dark threads

Hysteria

Skin translucent, veins divide blue to blue: the convenient comfort of fingers hiding eyes makes vision changeable. Untrustworthy. Knows no mind, the body. In cavernous happenstance, in uncertain dusk, in danger—the moment slips out of control. We require some subsequent, some *consequently*. Blame the physiology of equilibrium, that merciless truth: in the half-life of hand to wrist, that spectral longing, the clever body glows, refuses to comply. All you have to do is touch me. Meanwhile, we hold the chair's broken back accountable for our daily treachery, for breath in splinters. No matter what you wish for or how you want it: body body body, dumb and madly insubordinate. Meanwhile we softly, we signify, we linger like the blood that rings the nail bed. Unmistakable, the pattern can still catch us by surprise; we burn our impressions into beams, into brick. We have no other choice. This is the memory of events witnessed while sleepwalking. This is a language of tip and spill, in which each word means carefully. And when I think I'll suffocate? This is the necessary breath. We have no other.

Catalog and Lexicon

An unsympathetic ghost, demanding.

The Man on Whom Nothing is Lost lets go his tree-dark song in swirls around the house, the table tops, wild over endless acres and boats anchored in the narrow passage.

The sand and tide, the blooming garden, the bowls of yellow wine, every last bomb, and the shifting and fearful, the unearned confidence—these he gives the eldest. The youngest is bruised and fist-tight, unearthing her distance and her return.

Day and day and day thereby.

A spine-straight Lighthouse Man turns the prying beam out across the open, the sea thrown-wide.

Absent the first time, after the sudden slip, the sudden lost footing. Finds her in the end, weightless, following a most unlikely chain of events.

Says remember remember remember.

An ancient apotheosis of the shining sky; god of the elements, of rain, wind, thunder, lightning; stands atop a bald hill, mostly without brides.

Pours out the contents of his fantastic skull.

Always, always, always.

The Keeper of the Library of Appetites patiently collects our craving, keeps a detailed catalog of every thirst, every amazement.

He fills the dangerous gap between sleep and waking with gulp after sooty gulp of hot air and hot ash. The walls give way. Still he climbs in our estimation when we hear those loose bullets rattle in his pocket.

Begot, begot, begot.

The Fine Woodsman sends his children into the dismal forest, where the cottage, where the witch, where the oven.

Afraid, he sets the child upon a bough, no, upon a float; puts him right down in the course and rush and goes on. Or agrees to this.

The Little King of Everything knows the weight of our lungs and the scars marking fingers, arms, each contour, every uneven pink-white seam where skin split and came eventually together, all over again.

txt

letter by tarnished letter we can't
say more restless our momentary
messages collecting in phonelight
and the voice braids itself backward
a new silence pushes lexicon
to the brink I satisfy myself with
brevity and broken fingernails
and dusk like a slipknot drawn fades
answers unambiguous *I always*
and *you always* and *no* and *no*
and *no* little pleas diminish glow
faintly my petty resolutions cinder
and I crave shudder and chime
crave hands pulling hair
loose from its clip think
if I'd left the door propped open
I know longing begins quietly
to collapse not quite spent nearly
gone now let's admit it there's no
telling what we might have done

Aside

Photograph, the far off almost
forest, graygreen and humid. It is

possible. Photograph like a map,
or its legend. Confined. No matter

how often or foolishly. No wildness
in any direction, not for miles.

But I was talking about the pitiless door
stuck tight. About the moment

I throw my shoulder again against it,
the inconsequential standoff,

threshold holding me hasty,
distant in between.

Photograph: a theory of mishap; it tells us
nothing about the climate in this region.

Echo's Body

Echo still had a body then, she was not only a voice.

—Ovid

afternoon casts spiny certainties

into corners and it's clear

that I am or you are not

what the tree limbs predicted

in July-suspended air green and

promising storm violently

spectacular hot and furious

wind winding through houses

believe me I watched their secrets

catch in glow and tangle those

second-story nights headlights fell

into windows and there were horizons

in every dark direction alone at once

we waver and guess we reach across

across we know the secrets aren't

the interesting part the only part

tonight will be winter and we may

go under we may yet drown and here

in possibility's dim and quavering

strike I would peel skin from knuckle

and wrist I would give jawbone
or eyelid or tongue even now
the body articulates tremble and gasp
even now your hands drop through me

Little Winter Theater

January between us perfectly
ordered box, little winter theater,

tiny ambition: violet-blue violets,
palm-flat books, silver dollars,

and dolls with lips drawn tight
(don't you find it captivating, this

locking of the jaw?). Narrow
window—sparrows and wind

rising and finally snow; unlaced
shadows, the dread and sensibility

we reach across. Your hands
certain—immediate

flawless wrist, wrist—you lift
the box's bright curiosities:

one little book examines the complex
erotics of claustrophobia; one studies

the innocent murmur behind
once-broken, healed-crooked ribs.

II

Mnemonic

For the blessed Graces come the sooner to those adorned
with flowers and turn away from the ungarlanded.

—Sappho

Deep heavy rain leaves twisted
boneroots exposed; the tree can barely

hold itself.
                                Still now upright
limbs extend wishfully in a hundred directions.

— —

Awake midnight: opening
eyes scatter stars, free them
from their subtle rings and
                        send them staggering.

— —

the trees do not; we do not

— —

you said to me
you said to me
you said to me

you said

— —

Persistent as a cool thread
of wind slipping under a door.

— —

Buried yourself in echoes.

— —

To deck with flowers
twist weave tie flourishing
leaves to braid a fragrant crown;

this is what it means to want
almost past what can be endured.

— —

Awake midnight
to find the ghost
I half believe in
whispering
into my mouth

— —

We remember the suspended
landscape caught, banked,

hovering, a mirage lit and
held in bright and untenable space.

—— ——

Already, the body
reckless, extraordinary,
brass-bright with fearlessness;

the body becoming
invisible and sky-like.

Ring

tiny bell rant coincident near curve
wet sunlight negotiating sill and
chipped-paint ceiling a lesson by hint
and degree *I'll tell you why and there
was also winter* how you articulated
joint and turn voice like a memento
like a relic you whispered you supposed
and my discerning my resolute spine
understood I sat up to listen to longing
streaming in wire-seamed glass and then
and no not again the same sky-hollow
afternoon the single forgettable hour how
threadless and clean how I lost you finally
into the pocked mouthpiece of the phone
and now and nevertheless the receiver still
off the hook like our imagined old days
pushy signal droning like a true and
ancient word unfastened and yes I am
lucky in slanting shadow rigidly un-
voiced I am fixed and irrevocable I am
barely visible in this long-windowed room

Melancholia

A window imagines
remote constellations

and the moon resists each
association, *not like anything*

they compare it to.
I spend the night thinking

about gravity's grip on the bed,
the body. About the way

blood behaves, conscious
of *pulse*; counting. Habit

like pacing the vacant hallway.
In the dream you are holding me.

Then mornings flush radiant;
the phone will ring and be answered.

In our separate cities, we are always
talking. Traffic distant on two streets,

voice and idiom slip one to another
(you say *capacities*, say *caprices*).

Today half of everything drops
to the pavement. I think you mean

losing ground but you say *falling apart.*
There is a lapse. An aside. There is

a faraway thought, glimmering
impossible. Afternoon I call, hear

the machine the unchanging
tone and I wonder *what will I say.*

I spend all day thinking about my heart.
It's undeniable, the greed

with which the telephone rings and
goes on ringing. In the dream,

you enter the room, you open your mouth
as if you might speak. Wonder

then *what did I say.* As if you might call
or cry out. You open your mouth:

red lips pink tongue and
the shining white edges of every tooth.

On Seeing the Dead

The figure, the familiar
curve of shoulder,
a chance made available
and quite.

— —

But the truth is the eye
is flexible and not
to be trusted. It is
careless, without
reluctance—long
on desire, short on
particulars. Some-
times keen to ignore
the obvious.

— —

Like a prayer
to St. Jude for a win
at the track, the possibility
of the long shot coming in
over the favorite. 10 to 1.

— —

And
sometimes too I
am disappointed
by my hands,
their willingness
to loosen their grip.

Network, Constellation

screenlit and glowing word
by slippery word the toothy
demands tiresome flicker and all
this simulation discourse falling
flat pleading won't you without
a trace of cheekbone or lash
please and please and please and no
memory of creased heat metallic
shiver marching the spine
every moment rendered blank
and blinking or bound and
scripted almost routine steady
to the end out of sight saying
I want and I want more of everything
illuminated page tedious marks
the sender is only echo and
our distant pleasures constellate
radiant-cold far-flung stars
white and always heatless

Mercury Retrograde

trick of light a ghostly planet's
failure to turn its reversal
like your ring slipping
to knuckle like that specific
absence resolved recorded
replayed addressing no one
exactly still catching slowly
this press and shade and shade
the way we speak to one
another our remote and decisive
machine rapport not wide-eyed
or singular or slight and I
am of two minds I hesitate I
ask and find without warning the
midnight open window dreaming
this ordinary radiance spilling
brilliant losses and returns
your answer unswerving
from the urgent first it locates me
nameless in the planet's
forgetful gaze now unguarded
and unmistakable under

Mercury's perpetual spinning
its distant and indelible habit

Love Story

Scraped bloody, skin split
and the given fabric of twilight

coming away in ribbons. He is
a wound in the faroff; a key

in the lock, empty house resonant.
Whispered doorway appeal. Or a curse,

a trance, a fever vision dark with birds.
He is always already in the room

when she enters. A riot of chance: blackjack,
double down; or dice rattle, spin at the feet

of wretched men, (still wretched even now).
She is single-minded; he's a blindfold.

Dress

well-worn twilight demands

persistent sequence casual

hint and spine aligns

hesitate fasten hold taut

inch to inch whipstitched shift

caught to contour matched exactly

seam to seam the slide climbing

skin bare beneath and this

memory turning language

to silk precise and needful

Broken Rib

breath caught stiff now
interrupted by teeth by
lips breath stretched near
panting near sobbing cleft
bone announces obscure
and jagged crush and rupture
beneath burning skin blush-red
a tender appeal no hesitation
regardless lung's range muscle's
transaction flex or force and air
submits to suggestion rushes in fills
the break the certain aftermath
describes a critical seam

Roof

seventh-floor view and this
city so like itself so far from
gravity's promise this whim
simple idea glancing sidelong
or downward I am dry mouthed
and sullen as a child watching
sun collect along my edge
casting suggestion sequence
unavoidable next chance
meeting or private missive
the next tiny disaster open
my eyes at last and wonder
where you are speculate
your careless touch to cheek or
temple that concrete moment
I guess then at what you want
your absolute reply confounded
with certainty watching the tide
to mark duration I study
this untroubled Sound
observe every truth made
of many small decisions
one and one and one

Holograph

Surface and swirl, time's condition
shot through with pitchy revelation:

this is a history of lead. Cascade
confined, margin and page. Now

moss and sweaty air collect beneath
the tongue. It's true (a matter of fact):

reading a man's handwriting is like
looking at the shape of his mouth.

Snapshots

This captured doorway instant in which he prepares
to disappear. Worth a thousand words. It *developed*:
first under-leaf yellow, this flat singularity turned
distinct, glossy. Stopped time, then, like a snap of
fingers. As if it could be permanent, this second
when the rest of the story hadn't been told. Or it
tells a story, is a story. Backlit. About to turn. The
threshold and the day nearly over.

— —

What we said added up to amounts now to just more
than nothing: pale curves streaking the surface when
a car passes. Almost by heart your voice. One word,
perfect secret, the catch of it. Skipped behind my
ribs like a stone. Memory of craving: wantwantwant
and the mouth aches. The room has slipped my
mind, but the door. Fist poised, prepared to knock.
Already we understood the terms.

— —

Picture it. Color set seamed and drawn in ropy
waves, pigment ripples. Interior shade and cool.
Open door. Shutter. What's arrested is not our
graceless embrace, the kiss-on-both-cheeks instant.
Blooming atmosphere where he stands. Where he
is always standing, framed and framed. Expression

I can't make out. What's arrested, held up here in careful fingers: some sliver of a plot now faded past recall.

———

In the end, I played my awkward and underwritten supporting role with a kind of unexpected drunkenness and hip sway swagger. But at our best we spun words to tender webs, laced a glossed and sugary surface to cover whole nights in sweet translucence. Answers streaming, falling in strands. Then the ache in every limb was unmistakable; this stupid body, bare collarbone beckoning.

———

Finally I understood that there might as well have been a trapdoor. It occurred to me that he might be a fiction. Forgotten details burn, trouble the corner of the eye. Flash and blur. Parting, I concealed pitiless curiosity, my insatiable interest, in the curl of my fingers pressed firmly to his shoulder, in the blank where my lips nearly met his skin.

———

The man small enough now to rest in my palm. Every color, gathered or smooth or let loose to fray. Still present in the pattern. I could know everything this moment has to offer. Over exposure bleeds the edges white. Whatever else, there was collapsibility in that present, in this transparent present tense, plastic promise concentrated in trice, slanting radiance in flashpoint and flicker.

Ordinary Unhappiness

Haze drift hazy oblivion golden and
rippled by trace or guess and we

forget the pine-heavy coast lungful by
salted lungful forget not rocking into

sleep into waking; at sea it's possible
to crack open the chest to see the moonlit

heart still beating in its too-wide bonecage
its wet cavity, its insistent, its reckless dark.

The Nocturnal Factory

Caught in the crack separating one day from the next.

The first dreambreath aches in sleep-soaked lungs; it finds, in due course, one or another kind of focus: slips watery into moonlit view or surfaces from some depth like a panic.

Or a foot asleep: *pinsandneedlespinsandneedles.*

All winter I wrote everything down. I wouldn't have imagined I imagined such things.

Recurring: the near stranger I always recognize. His coarse form, a smell metallic, red as wine. Eyes grab at everything, even what I've hidden. Mouth designed to smother. His grip. He turns when I—

Or the swimmer will choke, drown, go missing among the rough oyster beds and their insufficient harvest. The light is oceanic, green, and barely light at all.

The clutch of it. The hold it has. A mysterious and vaporous power: the spherical capsule contains some volatile liquid for inhalation. Knock me knock me out.

Pry into the dream's body; lift its dense hot organs one by one and place them on the table. Slice each open. Record what you find there.

I risk listening again for more bits of the script. I didn't write this story and who knows how it ends. If I discover what I am expected to say. If I say it.

Wake and turn to the window. The view is cracks in pavement. Sightline to the end of the block. Nextdoor house lit even in the center of night's bleak revolution. None of this tells you much about who you love. And, in any case, eventually you lose your footing. Slip into the same sleep all over again.

In this way nights string themselves, iridescent pearls, flawless strand.

Again the painful breath of evening and the sleeper knows the time is coming. Will come.

Grieving Narcissus

sound decaying within the ear
and without your chaos memory
born of blue contemplation an eye
first revealing bones or that ever-
wavering reflection and how you are
exceptional again and I observe
your lips open around *oh, I see* and
naturally I want to reply but
the last lasting dream of tiny frogs
filling my unhinged mouth keeps me
aloft and alert and dressed in disquiet
when you say *green* as the story goes
you say *in this light* and *slantingly*
at the far edge of a fine afternoon but
it's been raining for days even in this
corner room where I waited and waited
where I heard almost every word

III

Midnight Continuous

unreachable city inevitable it shines

now again side-by-side we are

dashlit we are imagined anew

the unchanging view breathtaking

i.e. *air never decides if it first enters or*

leaves the lungs now this is also the past

where tenderly he hates me all over

all neon and blur a skyline a hemline

a faroff nearing the edge again

now the heart stunned static

my silent silent we're blinded

by passing headlights who wouldn't

lose sight our hours our hands

incessant so unequaled you are

familiar you are hipbone and brow

you are perfectly remembered

and perfectly indifferent

Night Swimmers

The window observes
the water's transactions

with the moon: seadark
proposal working

the scene to pieces. And
with that house lit fearsome

behind us, we crossed tide-
stained sand, sank to ankles.

The rule of unsteadiness says
the past is wild but almost

over. Clear-voiced Atlantic,
dizzy thrill. We walked into

that charmed cold; *follow*
said the water and we did.

Language of Mirrors

true if truly indifferent
stream from the faucet
a confirmation a gradual
seduction pooling in the sink
chlorine-bright a figment
by head by heart and likeness
has its own allure makes its own
demands the way fingers
give up their secrets in clumsy
silk unbuttonings now
I've forgotten what you said
about the echo chamber precision
of our speech because
the condition of this knowledge
is visual alone it's between us
lucid a concentration
polished relentless even
when the bulb blows
with a crack in the middle
of any night and I am see-
through and gleaming an image
exact or approximate and
clear as water from the tap

Hysteria

The rigid inside of the wrist, the exact origin of utterance.
Take nothing for granted. Air entering foundation the
shape of it: syllables illustrate meaning. Words the tongue
longs for. Day and night I handle ideas and objects (deny
myself this, allow myself this). Predictable grammar of
inadequacy: I see my shadow fall on the front steps and
think *All you have to do is touch me*. The very thing, dear
brilliant, dear stranger, the answer: marks on my arm
where the dog's teeth sunk in. The story I've been trying
to tell you ends like this: *When she was momentarily blinded
and could not recognize him, he offered her his hands*. After all, the
body knows something.

Waiting, with Prayer

Winter moon approximating
orange streetlight;

an empty lot, a car
idling. And a vibration

behind the eyes: *wait.*
The story of one night, its

furious appetite. Dazzling
this verge of decay,

blue smoke border cross
vivid to vivid to brink.

Save me from slip
and breakage, from this

volcano ash and steam.
O radio, save me.

And O tiny phone, flat
and shining and still,

O won't you?
Waiting,

head on fists, held up
against gravity, against

the weight of charms
that drag steadily and

always from the silver
chain around the neck.

Planetary Discourse

When you say *planet* it will be understood to mean *led astray* or *wander* or *the unavoidable catastrophe of detachment.*

Saturn is the opposite of Mercury; sight, the opposite of touch.

Greedy Wife, breathless as a ghost; and her singleness of purpose. She, mused to madness, bathed starwhite. And her Husband. O. The absolute force, the inevitability: she circles above, always at the same safe distance.

For all the bluster, all the shouting, all the sparks and swinging of iron and arms, the war in the end was rained out. Mars, after all, is only one god. There are so many others.

O, Guardian of Dust and Crop Circles; O, Protector of Earth-Brown Mysteries and Plow-Torn Stalks.

In this language there is one word that means both *wish* and *time.*

Not mist or like it. Not banded smoke. There are no colored gasses lighter than air and no wind currents to set them spinning. Celestial Ring: a Dense Swarm of Small Bodies.

One Goddess alone rules all the states of memory; hers is the economy of luck and stick and denial; you'll know her by her immaculate, her golden and glittering wings, the iridescent stitches of her gown.

The situation of heavenly objects, their orbits and relationships. And the satellites. And redlight bluelight yellowlight. Magnitude and physical condition. This is how we know where we end; where other tragedies begin.

Slender-armed Venus stands as still as a statue, glowing even in clear sunlight. Beautiful, of course, and the luckiest of all goddesses. The One at whom All Others Stare (scornful and envious). She is surprisingly like the moon.

The Astronomer and his elegant vocabulary remain mysterious, wrapped in milky distance; each planet, and he has hundreds, is represented by a distinct and separate sound.

Red, the Spring Canals thread straight across deep, but only at that time of year, when the water, when the rain, or the dust, or moon after moon after moon.

She will make another copper mirror and find herself in its burnt shine; she will not be kept from her own gaze.

In this language, it is it is impossible to say uppermost or unadorned or paradise.

If Breath is an Occasion for Memory

Underwater what the heart can do.
And the lungs—absentminded wish

like reaching for her, like saying her name.
Open to every watery or lucent, every

incomprehensible end: hands unfist and
the rushing to fill them. Sea sway unhurried;

dear devoted tide draw the long vowels out.
Painstaking articulation still every word is O.

Wherever you are, imagine the spent form turning
in the current like a song; imagine her hair.

Lapse

Night arrives hasty to the hook-and-eye sleeper.
The dark, it steals in. When I love you,

hornets circle my wrists in ropes of wing and
drone; angle of bone and bone, slip joint socket

muscled tight. Daybreak is turn of phrase
or point of view. Corrupt morning

will tell its lies—familiar, lavish. Like fire
or the threat of it, your reckless attention finds me

flushed and irrational. Vulnerable limb to limb,
to sting, to the predictable promise and burden

of fever: insight burns skin brilliant. See, I've been
thinking about the sometimes hitch in your voice;

thinking there are ways we understand seduction
that have nothing to do with the throat.

Between

Satellite, remote charm:
gray Mercury, pale circle.

Same planet rising,
inevitable over our

house. Newly ordered
quiet, half-lit:

what's between us.
Nightly, I trace patterns,

spectacular wanderings;
let evenings come

to nothing all on their own
(don't even try).

Hands pocketed,
empty of coin or

keepsake.
Horizon speculates, waits.

We worry ancient light
to the end of time.

Believe me, this is (it
passes for) devotion.

What I Thought When I Was Falling

possibilities of brutality
the icy red planet revolves
or night blazes with comets
oh yes when it broke open
the room when walls crashed
away in pieces then the sky
confirmed what was not
what had never been brick

Reckoning

> But Narcissus fled from her, crying as he did so, "Away with
> these embraces! I would die before I would have you touch
> me!" Echo's only answer was: "I would have you touch me!"
> —Ovid

your voice never wavered

same little words like fist

to back like a hard fall the air

knocked out still wanting

regardless I savor salt and bite

I tongue tiny cruelties praise

provisional gifts as the last

ringing hour resolves in bird spiral

swift into flight or

a moonless month of pleading

the moment imagines itself

back in time at once this is

how the body understands mouth

and breath knows the price

finally for giving any lie

a fair chance consequence

not wing to glass not palm

to clavicle but oh this dreadful

craving this predictable thrall the

lungs open and every kind of alive

Devotion

"What I desire I have," Narcissus cried. "My very plenty
makes me poor."
—Ovid

tell me will you and when

finally the last word rumored

and smokebound the truth

about this blurry and impatient

tenderness the ropy scars

it gradually leaves on lungs

Charms against the Ghost

On docks
On boardwalks
On dry wood and splinter

— —

And the bent crooked house
wasps' nest in the eaves, wings
in the chimney, chipped plaster
seams, the beams, the joints in the wall;

this enduring
house, this house
with its mouth sewn shut.

— —

Panic hums, lips pressed uneven:
mouth a twisted musicless crease.

— —

Burn the picture: emulsion blisters
blue then black, ash brittle and thin
flakes away on house currents;

old letters are also bad habits
and don't always burn easily
(you'd be surprised how long).

— —

Swallow
aspirin after

aspirin, the tiny
pink chalk baby

kind, but the
headache persists.

— —

Fingernails
tear stockings
to prove the skin
beneath;
        she
falls into it, this
habit of thinking
like a wife.

— —

(in the winter
dream of sewing

machines and
faintly-penciled

slanty-scripted
ransom notes

a pitchy dark
and darker

collection
of sparrows lift

together at once
as I pass)

— —

Unwrap the answer. Slip
its sticky revelation past
parted lips, tongue past teeth,
to sugary ache, to sweet
dissolution, to vanishing.

— —

On sidewalk and blacktop
On highways and highways

— —

Birds or leaves shadow
overhead like kites and

I'll whisper every secret
back into its bottle.

Nightly

Dream like a mouth open.
Inside the mouth.

Almost slipping notice,
tongue curves lip to

lip (the slightest reminder
burns brittle now or bright).

Consider my astonishment
when you reach for me.

In this room of broken throat
and glassy ache, yes,

there will be times
when I can't help myself.

I'll have the dream nightly;
I'll tell you everything.

NOTES

The title is from: Noah Webster, *An American Dictionary of the English Language*, 1828: "ECH'O, n. In fabulous history, a nymph, the daughter of the Air and Tellus, who pined into a sound, for love of Narcissus."

Poems titled "Hysteria," incorporate language from: Joseph Breuer and Sigmund Freud, *Studies on Hysteria*, 1895.

The last line in "Echo's Body" is from: Caitlin Mitchell, "taking hold," in *Hinge*, 2011.

The fourth section of "Mnemonic" is from an untitled collage by Allison McElroy, 2005.

"Melancholia": *not like anything they compare it to*... is from a haiku by Basho.

"Ordinary Unhappiness," takes its title from *Studies on Hysteria*: "...much will be gained if we succeed in transforming hysterical madness into ordinary unhappiness."

The italicized text in "Midnight Continuous" is from: D. W. Winnicott, "Primitive Emotional Development," 1945.

"If Breath is an Occasion for Memory," takes its title from: Susan Isaacs, "The Nature and Function of Phantasy," 1948.

AUTHOR

Nancy Kuhl is the author of *Suspend* (Shearsman 2010), *The Wife of the Left Hand* (Shearsman 2007), and several chapbooks. She is Curator of Poetry of the Yale Collection of American Literature at the Beinecke Rare Book and Manuscript Library. (www.phylumpress.com/nancykuhl.htm)

CPSIA information can be obtained
at www.ICGtesting.com
Printed in the USA
FFOW03n1812030215
10690FF

9 781848 614123